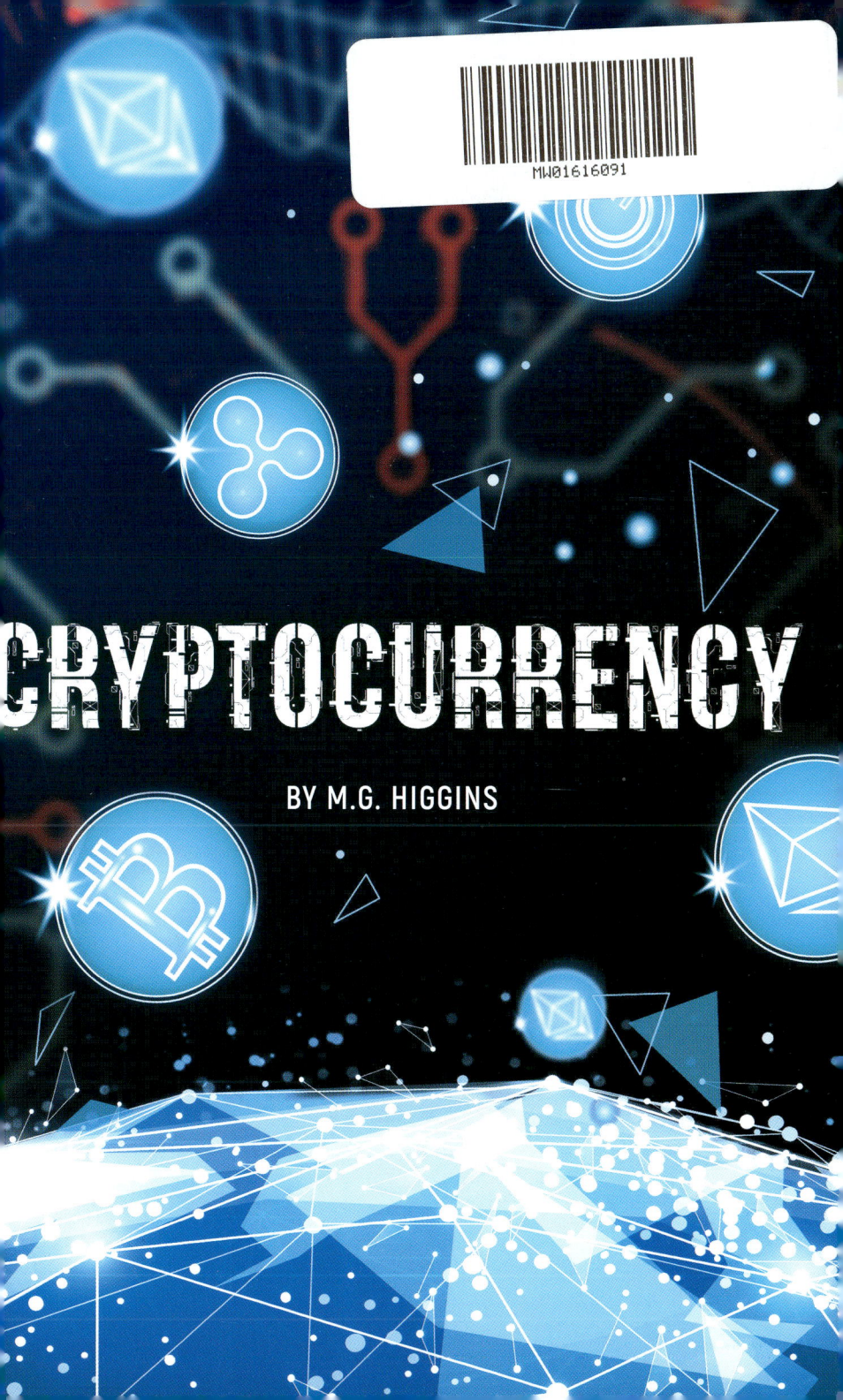

CRYPTOCURRENCY

BY M.G. HIGGINS

NONFICTION

Cryptocurrency

Deadly Bites

Droids and Robots

Flight Squads

SADDLEBACK
EDUCATIONAL PUBLISHING
www.sdlback.com

Photo credits: page 19: ARTYOORAN / Shutterstock.com; page 23: dennizn / Shutterstock.com; All other source images from Shutterstock.com

ISBN-13: 978-1-68021-638-7
eBook: 978-1-63078-475-1

Printed in Malaysia

23 22 21 20 19   1 2 3 4 5

Table of Contents

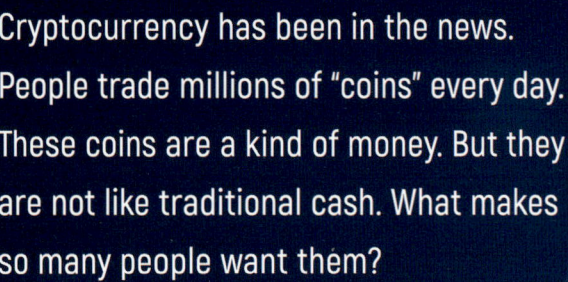

A Hot Topic

Cryptocurrency has been in the news. People trade millions of "coins" every day. These coins are a kind of money. But they are not like traditional cash. What makes so many people want them?

Digital Cash

Crypto is short for "cryptography." This is a code. It keeps data hidden. Currency is money. Cryptocurrency is a type of **digital cash**. It hides who uses it.

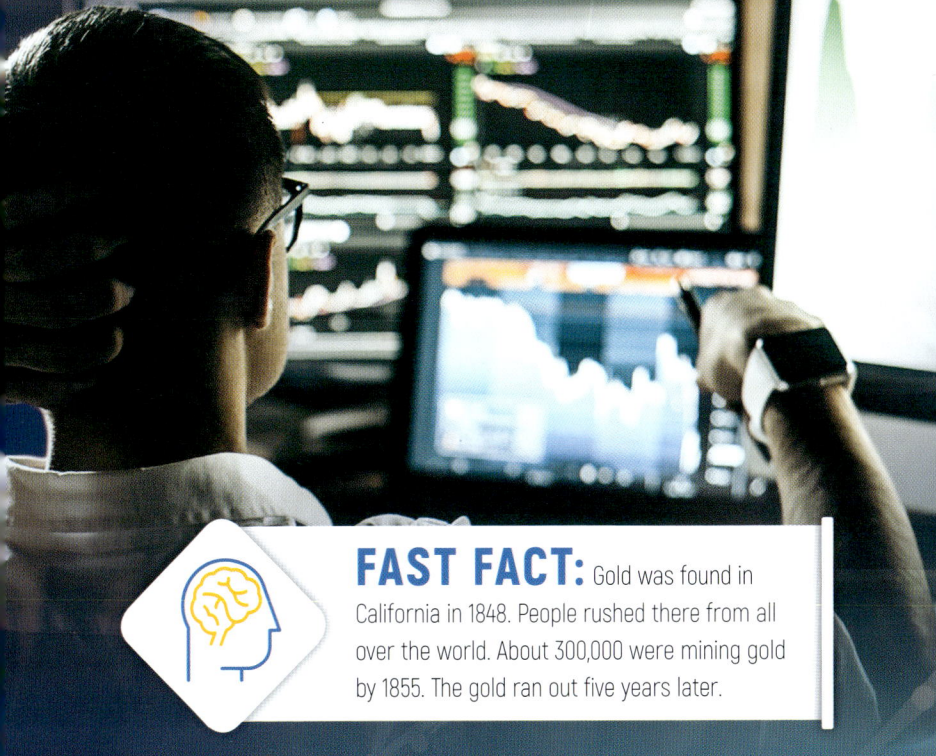

Digital cash is a kind of money. People buy things with it. They can invest in it too. But there are key differences. Cash is physical. People can hold it in their hands. Countries control it. Digital cash is not physical. Records are only online. No country controls it. Banks do not either. People do.

Some say it is like gold. This is because people mine for it. There is a kind of frenzy about it too. Many hope to get rich. It is like the Gold Rush of the 1850s.

Fraud or the Future?

There are people who like digital cash a lot. They think this is the money of the future. To them, it is safe and private. Some have made money with it.

Others do not trust digital cash. They say it is a fad. The coins have no real value. Some even call it a **fraud**. Warren Buffett is a money expert. He said digital cash ". . . will come to a bad ending." He swore he would never buy it.

FAST FACT: Bitcoin is the most well-known digital cash. There are many others. All use the same basic system.

No one knows what the future will bring. But digital cash may play a big part. It is changing how people think of money.

YOUNG MILLIONAIRE

Erik Finman turned 12. His grandmother gave him a gift of $1,000. He used the money to buy his first bitcoin. This was in 2011. Over time, Finman bought more. By the time Finman turned 19, he owned 401 bitcoins and was a millionaire. Finman tells young people to buy digital cash. But he also gives advice. Only invest what you are willing to lose. Experts give this advice too. Digital cash has shot up in price, and prices can sink just as fast.

Money Matters

People did not always use money. They traded. A person might have given someone a cow. They may have gotten corn in return. This changed over time.

The System Changes

It was 3,000 years ago. Metal coins came into use. They were worth the metal they were made of. Gold coins were common.

This system worked for thousands of years. Then something changed. Countries needed to pay for wars. There was not enough gold. They had to find another way. Paper money came into use. These bills were a kind of promise. Countries said the bills had value. People could use them like coins. But they could not trade bills for gold. That left more gold for the country to use.

FAST FACT: Some pictures show digital coins. But the coins are not real. They only exist online.

It was 1861. The U.S. started printing paper money. The money helped pay for the Civil War. Then the war ended. The U.S. chose to back its dollars with gold. This began in 1879. A person could go to a bank. They could get $100 of gold for a $100 bill. It was called the **gold standard**.

This changed in 1933. A law was passed. No one could keep gold without a permit. Then the policy ended.

It was 1971. The U.S. needed to print more cash. There was not enough gold to back it. Laws changed again. After that, money was just based on rules. A country said what it was worth. It is the same today.

Computers changed money even more. Today, people use credit cards. Some use online pay services. Others buy with apps. No bills or coins are touched. Money moves electronically. But it is still based on a country's currency. A **government agency** says what money is worth. In the U.S., that is the Federal Reserve. It is the U.S.'s central bank. Private banks are involved too. They hold people's money for them.

FAST FACT: Credit cards reveal personal data. Digital cash does not.

Concerns About Banks

Some say the system is broken. Central banks have too much power. Just a few people run them. But their decisions affect the world. Many say private banks have flaws too. They do not protect **privacy**. Banks are big business. Their main goal is **profit**. They charge fees. Banks also spend investors' money. They may make bad decisions.

BANKS AS MIDDLEMEN

Much of banking today is electronic. But this is not the same as digital cash. Banks act as middlemen. A person might want to transfer money to someone. The bank must do it for them. Banks control the money they keep. A bank can freeze a person's account. Digital cash is different. People control it themselves. They send money where they want.

Some have wanted change for a long time. They hoped for a new money system. It would avoid banks. No country would be in charge. The money would be safe. Personal data would stay private. Cryptocurrency was the answer.

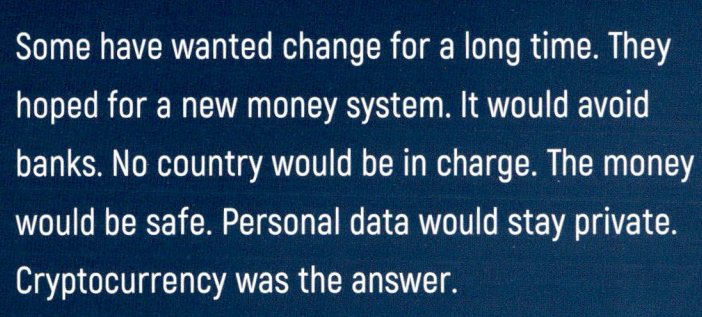

FAST FACT: People want privacy for a few reasons. They do not want personal data stolen. Some want freedom from a country's rules. Others trade in illegal goods. They want to avoid laws.

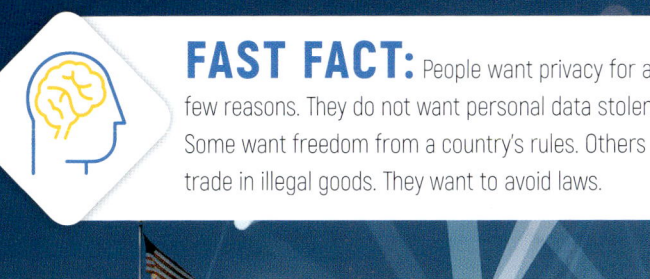

Bitcoin: The First Cryptocurrency

It was August 2008. A website appeared. The address was bitcoin.org. Two months went by. A paper showed up online. The author was Satoshi Nakamoto. This person wrote about a new cash system. It was called Bitcoin. No country would control it. It would not be tied to any bank. Money would move from person to person. Data would be in code. This would keep users private. Money transfers would be safe.

FAST FACT: No one controls digital cash. It works on its own.

It was January 3, 2009. Bitcoin software went online. The software was **open source**. This meant anyone could read it. A lot of coders read the paper. They looked at the software. Some liked what they saw. A few worked with Nakamoto. They fixed **bugs**. The program got better.

One of those people was Hal Finney. Finney was the first person paid with bitcoins. He got ten coins for his work. Bitcoins had no value back then. How did that change? A seller had to accept them. It would show what a coin was worth. That happened in 2010. A store took bitcoins. It was a pizza shop. A coder paid 10,000 bitcoins for two pizzas. Bitcoin gained trust. A few more places took it. The coin's value went up ten times in 2010.

FAST FACT: The bitcoins spent on that pizza in 2010 were worth $100 million in 2017.

WHO IS SATOSHI NAKAMOTO?

Nakamoto stopped working on Bitcoin in 2011. He sent an email. It said he had "moved on to other things." Then he vanished. This person is still a mystery. The name is likely fake. It could be one person. It could be a group of people. Some say it does not matter. Others say it does. Nakamoto owns about one million bitcoins. That is 5% of the total. The market could be flooded with them. That would sink the price of all bitcoins.

Gaining Attention

Then came 2011. The **Silk Road** began using bitcoins. This was a site on the **dark web**. People traded illegal items there. Bitcoins were an ideal way to pay. User information was kept private. Governments did not know who was buying or selling. **Demand** for the coins grew. Value jumped to $10 per coin.

The coin's worth went up even more in 2012. People began buying bitcoins as an investment. They hoped the coins would grow in value.

THE SILK ROAD

There was an earlier Silk Road. This one was thousands of years ago. It was an ancient network of international trade routes. Silk, spices, foods, animals, and more were traded from China to Greece as merchants traveled along these routes with their goods.

Other changes took place. More stores took the coins as payment. The first ATM for bitcoins was made in 2013. Users could trade bitcoins for cash. The Silk Road was shut down the same year. The U.S. Senate had hearings about it. The subject of digital cash came up. Bitcoin was in the news. It became hot. The price of one coin jumped to $1,242.

FAST FACT: People do not have to use a whole bitcoin. They can use "bits." The smallest is called a satoshi. It is worth a hundred millionth of a bitcoin.

Altcoins

Bitcoins were a big hit. Other digital coins soon followed. They are called **altcoins**.

Standing Out

Most altcoins start with Bitcoin software. Then the coin company tries to do something new. They want buyers to notice them.

Altcoins go by many names. Ripple is one. Steem is another. There are more than 1,000. Many are unknown. Few people buy them. But some stand out. Litecoin is one. It is faster than Bitcoin. Trades are quick. Another is Etherium. The coins are called Ether. It is also faster than Bitcoin. Some fees are lower too.

FAST FACT: Some coins are called tokens.

Rising in Value

Altcoins have been around a few years. Many have gone up in value. More than half went up 300%. Some have gone even higher. They were worth about $78 billion in 2017. One reason for the big jump was cost. Bitcoins are expensive. Few can afford them. But people like the idea of digital cash. They want to invest. Most altcoins cost less. Many are under a dollar.

There are some downsides. Altcoins can be hard to spend. Few sellers take them. Some are hard to buy too. Not all markets trade them. More than 600 altcoins have failed. Many were **scams**. They took bitcoins as payment. Then the founders quit, running off with the money. Other scams planted hacking software. These stole personal data. Altcoins have failed for other reasons. The coins were not special. Buyers were not interested.

BUYING COINS

Millions of people own digital cash. Most get it from exchanges. These are services. People use them to buy and sell coins. They are only online. Coinbase is a big one. Kraken is another. They make money from fees. This can be up to 1% of the purchase price. Most exchanges trade in bitcoins. They do not carry all altcoins.

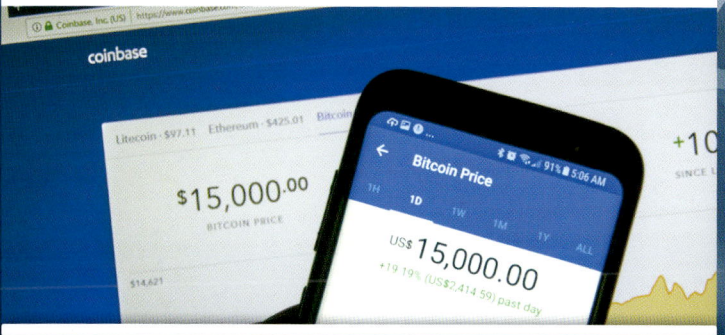

FAST FACT: Bitcoin bits are cheaper than full bitcoins. But some people do not know they can buy them. Others only want full coins.

The Basics

Digital cash can be used like real money. Coins have value. They can be used to buy things. But how they work is different.

Money is a real object. Digital coins are not. They are only online. This can cause problems. Here is an example. Kim has one dollar. She gives it to her friend Lee. The two friends know the transfer took place. Kim handed the money to Lee. But what if the dollar is digital? How does Lee know if it is really his? Maybe Kim gave it to someone else. Perhaps she made copies of the bill. Those might have been given to others.

Blocks and the Blockchain

Trust was a big problem. Experts worked on this for a while. Then Bitcoin solved it. They made blocks. These are online lists. All transfers go on them. The blocks are joined together. This makes an even bigger list. It is called the **blockchain**. This has the history of all transfers.

FAST FACT: The blockchain is also called the public ledger.

Think of Kim's digital dollar. Her transfer gets added to the blockchain. It says the dollar went to Lee. But Lee is still not sure. Kim might have cheated. She could have made a fake entry. The blockchain might say Kim gave the dollar to Stan. It might say Kim gave three dollars to Lee. How can Lee know?

FAST FACT: A Bitcoin transfer can take up to an hour or more. That includes mining. Most altcoin transfers go much faster.

Experts solved this problem too. They made the blockchain public. Anyone can see it. Users are part of a network. They compare their lists. All must match. This makes it very hard to cheat.

NETWORKS

Networks are key to how digital cash works. They are made up of all users. Users run the same software. Their computers talk online. This kind of network has a name. It is called peer-to-peer. The nickname is P2P. Special computers are in the network. These are called nodes. A transfer of digital cash starts with them.

How a Bitcoin Transaction Happens

STEP 1:
Both Kim and Lee have Bitcoin wallets installed on their computers.

STEP 2:
Kim sends a message to Bitcoin that she wants to send money to Lee. She uses her public key and Lee's public key.

STEP 3:
Kim signs her request with her private key.

STEP 4:

Special computers called nodes analyze the request to make sure it is okay.

STEP 5:

Miners begin to process the request, which is part of a block.

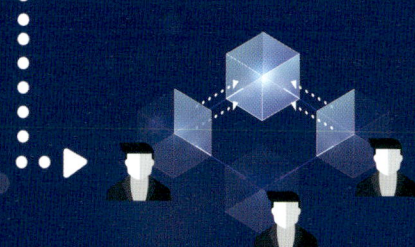

STEP 6:

One of the miners completes the request, and the block is added to other blocks.

STEP 7:

The money transfer is completed, and the block is visible in the blockchain. This is public, so anyone can view it.

6 Using Digital Cash

Computers check everything. The data has to match. Then digital cash is okay to spend.

Many people keep money in wallets. Digital cash users do the same. But these wallets can be online. Computers have them. Smartphones do too. Each wallet holds two keys. These are codes with letters and numbers. One is private. It belongs to a person. The other is public. It is used to transfer coins. Anyone can see it.

Here is how a transfer might work. Jeff wants to buy a new car. He finds a seller who takes digital cash. Jeff sends a note to the network. It looks like this:

I am Public Key 193Sh5LWc89NQLpaxVeziUExcn8RHrB3J4. Please transfer 1 (one) coin to Public Key 2N8gxtiN8SgcEgFWhLwS4rslRhcxowPjTg.

Jeff signs the request. He does this with his private key. That shows the request came from him.

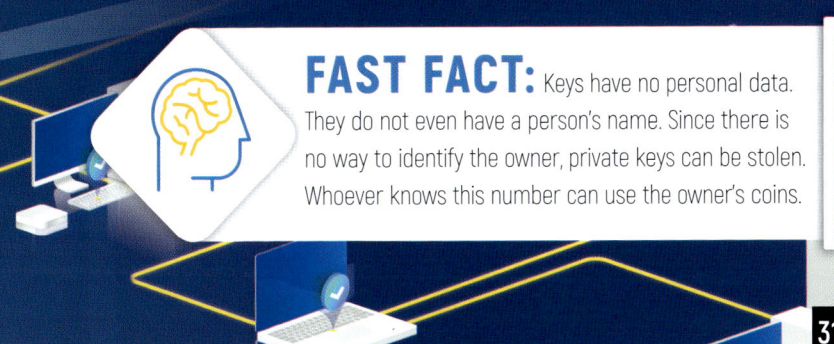

FAST FACT: Keys have no personal data. They do not even have a person's name. Since there is no way to identify the owner, private keys can be stolen. Whoever knows this number can use the owner's coins.

Nodes Do a First Check

The request goes to special computers. They are called **nodes**. These are part of the network. The nodes connect with Jeff's wallet. They compare Jeff's data to the blockchain. The blockchain has the history. It shows all past transfers. Coin balances are there too. The nodes agree. Things look fine. Jeff has enough money. His request is valid. Now it moves to the next step: mining.

FAST FACT: Transfer requests go to about eight nodes. Software chooses them at random.

CHAPTER

7

Mining for Coins

Miners are the backbone of the network. They have two main jobs. One job is to build the blockchain. The other is to create new coins.

Confirming Blocks

Think back to Jeff. He still has to pay for the car. The nodes have done their work. Jeff's request goes back into the network. Miners pick it up. They group the request with other valid requests. This is called a block. It might have 2,000 requests in all. Now a miner confirms the block. This makes the transfer permanent. It cannot be changed.

Mining is done in a certain way. Each block contains a math puzzle. The puzzle is tricky. Only special software can solve it. A miner solves the puzzle. This confirms the block. The miner sends proof back into the network. Nodes check the work. They make sure rules have been followed. Now the block becomes part of the blockchain. The transfer is done. Jeff's payment is complete.

FAST FACT: Computers that mine are called miners. People who own them are called miners too.

Reward in Coins

Mining is costly. Computers are not cheap. They use a lot of power. Electricity costs money too. There is competition. Miners race each other. The first to confirm a block gets coins. This is why they are called miners. It is like digging for gold.

It was 2009. A Bitcoin miner's reward was 50 coins. By 2018, it dropped to 12.5 coins. Around 2020, it will be 6.25 coins. This is part of Bitcoin's plan. The reward is cut in half with each 210,000 blocks. It is how Bitcoin counts down to its last coin. Some altcoins work the same as Bitcoin. Others do not reduce the reward.

MORE MINING INCOME

Miners verify blocks. Their reward is new coins. Miners make money another way. They collect fees. Users pay miners to make transfers. These fees can add up. Bitcoin miners got $2.3 million in transfer fees. This was for just one day in August 2017.

FAST FACT: The coins miners get are brand-new. This is how the currency grows.

Big Business

Many people want to mine. High costs are a challenge. But there are ways to keep costs down. Some people join mining pools. Miners work as a team. They share gear and split profits. Not all methods are legal. Some miners steal electricity. Others **hijack** personal computers. They even take over smartphones.

CAP ON COINS

Bitcoin set a cap on its coins. There will only ever be 21 million. That cap will be reached around 2040. The limit serves a purpose. It makes the coins rare. In this way, they are like gold. Some altcoins set similar limits. Others do not. One of these is Etherium. It releases a set amount on a regular basis. The supply keeps growing. It is more like dollars than gold. Experts are not sure which is better. Both work fine for now. But time will tell.

FAST FACT: Bitcoins were first mined on regular computers. Now computers are built just for mining. Many are housed in big data centers. More than 50% of these centers are in China.

Drawbacks

There are positive aspects of digital cash. The system runs itself. It does not need banks. Personal data stays safe. It can be used around the world. But it is not perfect. There are some big concerns.

High Fees

People pay a fee to transfer digital coins. It goes to the miner who confirms the block. Bitcoin fees started out low. Most were just a few cents. That changed over time. Fees were as high as $26 in 2017.

One reason for the rise is demand. More people are buying bitcoins. There are more transfers. The block system gets clogged. Miners charge more for faster service. Many users are not happy with this. Some are switching to altcoins. Most altcoins have lower fees. But demand for them is going up too. Their fees may rise.

Big Price Swings

Digital cash is **volatile**. This means prices rise and fall quickly. Bitcoin lost 30% of its value in one day. That was December 22, 2017. It started at a high of $19,500. Then it fell as low as $11,000. A bitcoin was worth about $6,000 a month later.

NEW LAWS?

People like digital cash. It is private. Personal data stays safe. But this has a downside. Criminals like it too. It keeps them hidden. Some use it to make drug deals. They use it to process stolen money. Countries have taken notice. Vietnam has banned digital cash. The United Kingdom plans to control it. The U.S. may do the same. Banks are unhappy with digital cash too. It could put them out of business. They urge countries to clamp down.

Bitcoin Value Swings Wildly December 2017

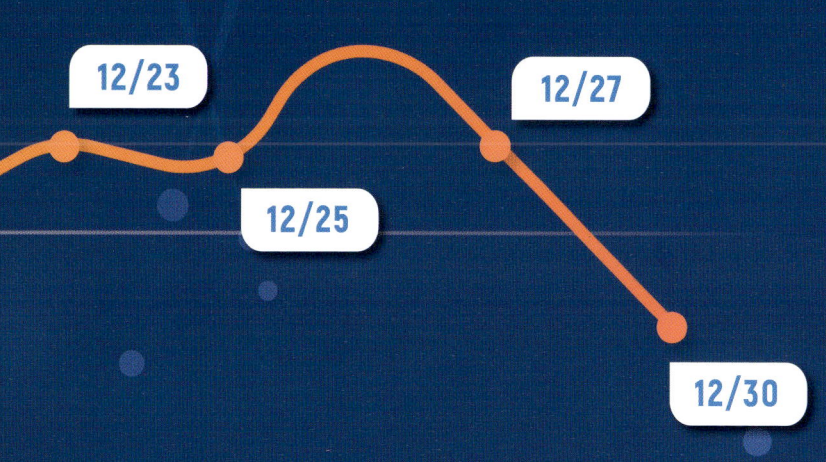

12/23

12/25

12/27

12/30

Altcoins swing in value too. There are a few reasons for these shifts. One is fear. Countries say they want to control digital cash. This scares users. They prefer no controls. Big hacks scare users too. But digital cash is still growing. People want in on it. Demand keeps prices rising.

Price swings impact stores too. Think about this. A buyer makes a purchase. The coin's value drops an hour later. The store loses money. That is one reason few stores take it. Other stores take a chance. Buyers want to use digital cash. Taking it is a way to attract them. The price could shoot up too. Then the store would make extra money.

FAST FACT: A lot of hijacked computers mine for one altcoin. It is called Monero. This coin is more secure than Bitcoin. Users are harder to track.

Hijacked!

Mining for digital cash is a big draw. But it costs a lot. Criminals work around this. They hijack computers. Over 500 million people mine coins. They do not even know it.

One of every 40 websites has this **malware**. A person opens a web page. Mining software connects to their computer. Then it runs in the background. The person has no idea. Victims live all over the world. But most live in the U.S.

Big Hacks

Fans claim digital cash is safe. This is true in some ways. Networks can be hard to hack. They are very secure. But hackers have found other ways.

Hacks

Networks may be safe. But online wallets are not. Hackers like to target them. The first hack was in 2011. A man kept his wallet online. Hackers got into it. They stole about $250 million in coins. Wallet services are at risk too. These hold onto people's coins. One was MyBitcoin. It was hacked in 2011. All its coins vanished.

Coin exchanges are at risk. They have had some of the biggest hacks. Bitfloor was one of the first. It was hacked in 2012. About 24,000 bitcoins were stolen. One of the worst hacks was in 2014. Mt. Gox was the world's biggest exchange. About 850,000 bitcoins went missing. Since then, many more coin exchanges have been hacked.

FAST FACT: The safest place for a wallet is offline. Some people keep them on flash drives.

Ransomware

Some hackers use **ransomware**. This is a kind of malware. It locks computer files. People must pay to get them unlocked. Hackers will release the files. But they want money first. Hackers wanted real money in the past. Now many want digital cash. An attack struck San Francisco. This was at the end of 2016. The target was the city's subway. Hackers demanded 100 bitcoins.

FAST FACT: All kinds of digital cash have been hacked. Bitcoin has been hit the most. It is the oldest. Bitcoin is worth the most too.

A global attack hit in May 2017. The software was called WannaCry. It struck about 200,000 computers. The ransom was $300 in bitcoins. More than 200 victims paid. The attacks were linked to North Korea.

SPENDING STOLEN COINS

A person's wallet is stolen. The thief now has their private key. They can spend the victim's coins. But using stolen coins is not easy. There is special software. It can track bitcoins and some altcoins. Police use it to find who spends them. Some arrests have been made. Now hackers have changed tactics. They focus on safer altcoins that hide private data better. Hackers use mixers too. These are special exchanges. Stolen and clean coins are mixed. These are harder to track.

10 The Future

Digital cash is still new. Not all are sure it will survive. There is hope for this new technology. There are also challenges ahead.

Other Uses for Blockchains

The blockchain system keeps perfect records. It keeps data safe. There are many uses besides money. One idea is smart contracts. These can be programmed. They can tell when a condition is met. This could be a certain date. Then the contract takes its next step. That might be releasing funds. People would not control contracts. Computers would.

Not all voters vote in elections. Online voting is one answer. But there is a big hang-up. Online votes can be hacked. Blockchains could change that. Voters could see their votes being cast. Voters themselves would stay private.

People have many IDs. A credit card is one. A passport is another. Hackers can find this data online. Keeping it safe is a big problem. Blockchains can help here too. People would use keys. No passwords would be needed. User data could stay offline.

Coin Dumps

A few people have a lot of digital cash. Just 4% of users own 95% of all bitcoins. Just 1% control half of the Bitcoin market. This was in 2018. These users are called whales. Altcoins have whales too. These people worry other users. One or more whales might sell all their coins. These coins would flood the market. The value of all coins would drop. They might become worthless.

FAST FACT: Some people buy a lot of one coin. The buyers want its value to rise quickly. Then they sell for a big profit. This scam has a name. It is called pump and dump.

Using the World's Energy

Mining uses power. Each day, miners confirm more blocks. More coins are created. Experts say mining will keep burning more power. Soon it will use more power than the U.S. uses today. That will jump to all the world's power by 2020.

People are looking for answers. One is new software. It will confirm blocks in a different way. Another is a new system. Miners will not solve math puzzles. They will do something else. One city has an idea. They want to use the exhaust from data centers. It will heat homes. The heat could be turned into electricity too. Some say none of this will matter. Digital cash is sure to fail. Mining will stop any day now.

Is digital cash the money of the future? Some say it is. They hope this radical change is here to stay. Others say it is just a fad. The bubble will soon burst. Time will tell who is right.

BITCOIN IN 2040

The last bitcoin will be mined around 2040. It could be sooner. That is when the cap of 21 million coins is reached. Some say that will be the end of Bitcoin. Others say it will still be around. Miners will no longer earn new coins. But they will still earn transfer fees. Some experts think this will be enough to keep it going.

Glossary

altcoin: digital currency that is similar to a bitcoin

blockchain: a digital log of all cryptocurrency transactions that is publicly available

bug: an issue that keeps a computer program from working the way it is supposed to

coin exchange: a digital marketplace for buying and selling cryptocurrency

dark web: a part of the internet that can only be accessed using special software; users are not able to be identified or traced

demand: the need for something

digital cash: money that can be sent to or received from another person electronically

fraud: a crime where someone falsely represents themselves in order to steal from another person

gold standard: the system that determined the value of currency in terms of gold because that is what money could be exchanged for

government agency: a group of people who are part of the government and work together in an official capacity

hijack: to take control of

malware: software that has been created to damage or take over computers

node: a computer that is part of the blockchain network and is used to verify cryptocurrency transactions

open source: software code that is available for all to use and change as needed

privacy: being free from being watched or monitored by others

profit: money that is made through business transactions

ransomware: a type of software that is designed to take over a computer until money is paid

scam: a way to get people's money by lying to them

Silk Road: an online market where people bought and sold illegal goods on the dark web; this was shut down in October 2013 by the FBI

volatile: likely to make big changes quickly

DROIDS AND ROBOTS

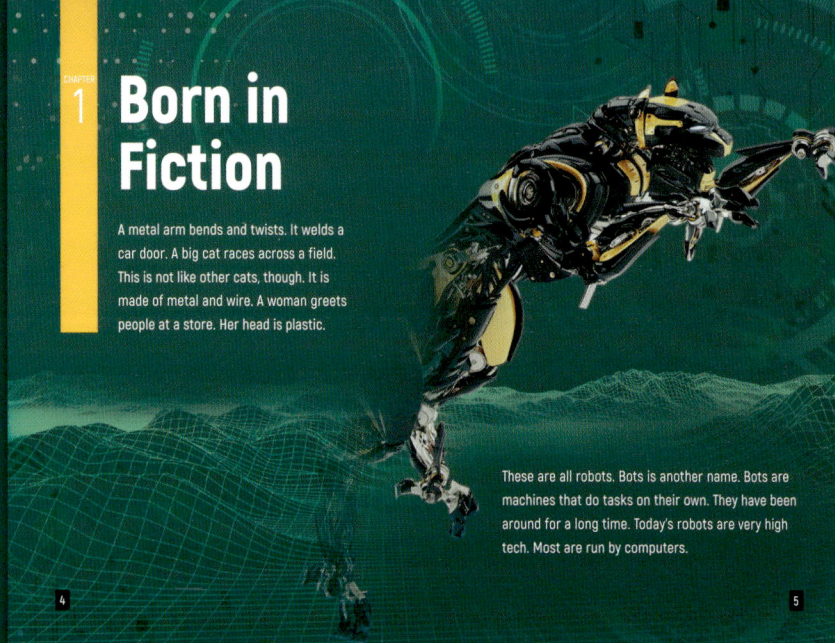

Born in Fiction

A metal arm bends and twists. It welds a car door. A big cat races across a field. This is not like other cats, though. It is made of metal and wire. A woman greets people at a store. Her head is plastic.

These are all robots. Bots is another name. Bots are machines that do tasks on their own. They have been around for a long time. Today's robots are very high tech. Most are run by computers.

Answers

Bots do help people in many ways. Job loss is real, though. What can be done? One answer is schools. There are jobs to fill now. More will come in the future. The tasks have just changed. Robots need to be built. They need repair. All must have software. These jobs take special skills. Math is key. Science is too. Many say schools need to focus more on these subjects.

Some experts point to history. New tech waves result in job loss. This happened in the 1800s. Then came computers in the 1970s. Jobs were lost again, but that did not last. New jobs were created. Many jobs people never predicted. A future with robots may be the same.

Likelihood of Jobs Going to Robots

PREDICTABLE PHYSICAL WORK

78% Routine jobs, like working in an assembly line, preparing food, and packing boxes are more likely to go to robots.

UNPREDICTABLE PHYSICAL WORK

Jobs where there is more change in tasks, such as construction and forestry are less likely to go to robots. **25%**

CHAPTER
10 Wave of the Future

Robots will get smarter. They will need less human control. People will depend on them more. Androids will even go to Mars.

Robonauts

Robots are in outer space now. They will play a key role in the future. NASA is the U.S. space agency. A team there is making robonauts. These are robots that are made to work in space. One is called R2. It works on the U.S. space station. R2 does work that is too risky for humans.

Today, there are seven robots on Mars. They take photos and collect samples. NASA plans to send androids there too. The R5 is being tested now. It is six feet tall and weighs 290 pounds. A group of them will go ahead of people. They will set up a station. All will then work together with humans.

WHITE LIGHTNING BOOKS®

NONFICTION

9781680216387

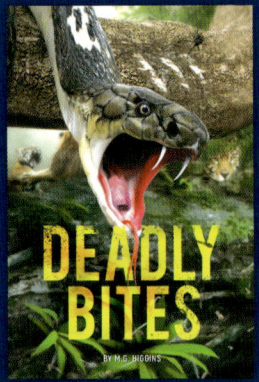

9781680216400

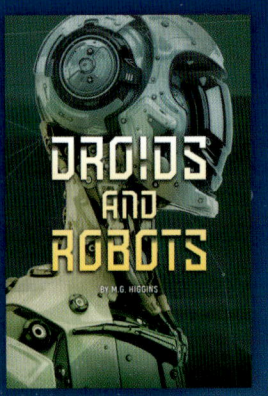

9781680216394

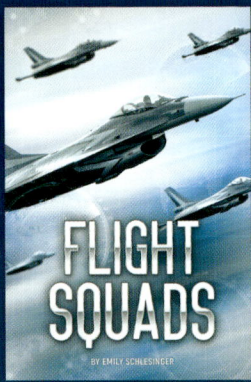

9781680216912

MORE TITLES COMING SOON
SDLBACK.COM/WHITE-LIGHTNING-BOOKS